WORLD ISSUES

NATURE VS MAN

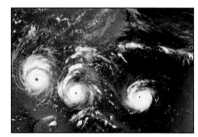

A look at the way the world is today

Antony Mason

Franklin Watts
London • Sydney

ABOUT THIS BOOK

NATURE vs MAN looks at the eternal problem that natural disasters pose for mankind. Although natural disasters have been a feature throughout history, our growing population is bringing more people into potential contact with catastrophic events. We have found ways to predict some natural disasters and to minimise their effects. But while we try to make natural disasters less devastating, human development is also causing greater destruction by damaging the environment. In the coming years, we must learn to work with nature, not against it.

© Aladdin Books Ltd 2006

Produced by
Aladdin Books Ltd
2/3 Fitzroy Mews
London W1T 6DF

ISBN 0–7496–6267–0

First published in 2006 by

Franklin Watts	Franklin Watts Australia
338 Euston Road	Hachette Children's Books
London	Level 17/207 Kent Street
NW1 3BH	Sydney NSW 2000

Designer: Flick, Book Design and Graphics
Editor: Katie Harker
Picture Research: Alexa Brown

The author, Antony Mason, is a freelance editor, and author of more than 60 books for both children and adults.

The consultant, Rob Bowden, is an education consultant, author and photographer specialising in social and environmental issues.

Printed in Malaysia   All rights reserved

A CIP catalogue record for this book is available from the British Library.
Dewey Classification: 363.34

CONTENTS

3

INTRODUCTION

Humans have always tried to control their environment, but they live alongside nature – a force more powerful than anything that man has ever created. Nature shaped and shook the Earth for millions of years before human life even existed. Natural disasters can flatten homes, kill people and wreck the lives of any survivors. We are unlikely to ever control the forces of nature, but we are beginning to learn how best to cope with them.

A MATTER OF STATISTICS

Humans have a very self-centred approach to natural disasters. We rate disasters in terms of the number of human deaths and casualties. This is what hits the headlines – an earthquake or volcanic eruption in a remote area is not considered particularly newsworthy. Instead, the human element determines whether a natural event becomes a disaster. The economic cost, particularly in more developed economies, is also a significant indication of the scale of a disaster for the governments concerned. As we move forwards in the 21st century, the population of the world is rising and natural disasters will inevitably affect greater numbers of people in the future. This expanding population is also likely to provoke certain kinds of natural disaster due to the impact that our daily lives have on the environment.

Trying to explain natural disasters

For the individuals involved, the scale of a disaster is irrelevant – the personal effects are always devastating. But natural disasters have always been a part of human life, and since the beginning of history, humans have struggled to

4

The world population is rising, and because we rate natural disasters in terms of statistics, the effects of nature are set to get worse in the future.

explain them. In the past, most people believed that natural disasters were sent by their gods to teach them some kind of lesson – and many people still believe this today. But in recent centuries, the scientific reasons behind natural disasters have become better understood. This has led to a greater understanding about how disasters occur, and increasingly advanced technology has made it possible to predict what might happen in the future.

Through equally advanced technology, news of a disaster spreads quickly, making it possible for rescue teams and aid workers to get to the scene within hours in some cases. This helps to reduce the suffering of the victims. But by the same token, disasters rapidly become sensational news stories, focusing on casualties. This can lead to a loss of perspective. Natural disasters may be tragic events, but they are seldom as destructive as other longer-term causes of death, such as disease and war, that do not grab as much media attention.

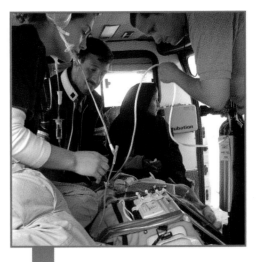

News of a natural disaster can spread very quickly. Sometimes, rescue teams attend to a scene within hours. The media coverage, however, can often divert attention away from longer-term problems, such as disease and war.

Ten of the worst natural disasters since 1881

	Approximate death toll	Type	Place	Date
1.	3 million	Flood	Huang He and Yangtze Rivers, China	1931
2.	1.5 million	Flood	Huang He and Yangtze Rivers, China	1887
3.	500,000	Cyclone / flood	Bhola, Bangladesh	1970
4.	300,000	Cyclone	Haiphong, Vietnam	1881
5.	280,000	Tsunami	Indonesia / Thailand / Sri Lanka / India	2004
6.	242,000*	Earthquake	Tangshan, Hebei Province, China	1976
7.	200,000	Earthquake	Qinghai, Gansu Province, China	1927
8.	200,000	Flood	Shanghai / Yangtze River, China	1911
9.	180,000	Earthquake	Xining, Gansu Province, China	1920
10.	160,000	Earthquake	Southern Italy and Sicily	1908

*This is the official figure, issued by the Chinese government. Outside sources suggest that the total may have been far higher, possibly 750,000 deaths.

These statistics do not include disasters in which deaths were caused by famine or epidemics alone.

WHAT IS A NATURAL DISASTER?

Any major event that causes widespread human damage (which is not directly caused by the actions of man) is described as a natural disaster. The event may injure or kill humans, or may simply damage their property. A volcanic eruption on an uninhabited island in the Pacific Ocean is not usually considered to be a natural disaster. But it might be, if the eruption inflicts exceptional damage on wildlife, or affects human life in some way (such as air-borne debris causing noticeable changes in the climate, for example). The main natural disasters are caused by an instability of the Earth's crust or by adverse weather conditions.

Some of the greatest damage is caused by ferocious weather (above) and movement in the Earth's crust (left).

THE RESTLESS EARTH

Ever since its creation 4.5 billion years ago, the Earth has been an unstable ball of rock. Its thin crust has been constantly rocked by earthquakes and volcanic eruptions, as its plates – into which the surface of the Earth is divided – push together and pull apart under massive pressure, in the unending process that we call plate tectonics.

This pressure may result in a sudden jolt, causing the ground to shake violently in an earthquake. The force of an earthquake is measured using the Richter scale. This is a logarithmic scale which means that 7 on the Richter scale (the force of a nuclear bomb) is ten times more powerful than 6 and 100 times more powerful than 5 (relatively mild). If an earthquake occurs in a built-up area, it is liable to cause massive devastation: houses will crumble, electricity cables and gas and water pipes will break, and roads, bridges and tunnels will collapse. Really big earthquakes are among the most deadly of all natural disasters: the one that occurred in Pakistan and Pakistani Kashmir in October 2005 (7.6 on the Richter scale) killed over 80,000 people. The most devastating earthquake ever, hit the city of Tangshan in China in 1976 (see page 5). This measured about 7.8 on the Richter scale.

6

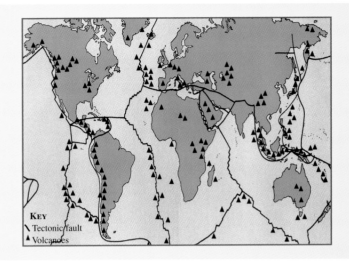

Tectonic plates

In the 1960s, geologists found a way to explain why some parts of the world suffer more from earthquakes and volcanoes: the Earth's surface is divided into a set of massive 'tectonic plates'. These plates fit together like a jigsaw puzzle, forming both the land and the ocean floors. The unstable mass of molten rock beneath the surface of the Earth causes the plates to move above it, like giant rafts. In some places the plates are pulling apart. Most earthquakes and volcanic eruptions occur where the plates collide or rub together.

KEY
\ Tectonic fault
▲ Volcanoes

Volcanic eruptions

Meanwhile, the liquid rock (magma) beneath the Earth's surface also tries to force its way up through the crust. When the magma comes across a weak spot, a volcano occurs. Some volcanoes release the pressure slowly in continuous eruptions of soft lava; others build up huge pressure beneath a hard plug of rock in the cone of the volcano before erupting in a gigantic explosion. This kind of eruption occurred at Vesuvius in AD79, burying the Roman cities of Pompeii and Herculaneum and killing some 3,500 people. More recently, in 1980, Mount St Helens in Washington State, USA, exploded, pulverising the top 400 metres of the mountain and devastating the landscape to the east. However, only 57 people died because the blast zone covered a forested area that was not heavily built-up. The area had also been evacuated.

A volcanic eruption can have other repercussions. In 1991, multiple eruptions at Mount Pinatubo, in the Philippines, caused the entire region to become covered in a deep carpet of damp volcanic ash and mud. An effective evacuation from the neighbouring cities brought 200,000 people to safety before their homes were crushed, but around 1,000 people died. The people of Armero in Colombia were not so fortunate; when Nevado del Ruiz erupted in 1985, a huge mudslide caused by volcanic activity came hurtling down the mountain and engulfed their town, killing 21,000 of the 23,000 inhabitants.

7

The eruption of Mount St Helens in 1980 killed 57 people. In addition, 200 homes, 47 bridges, 24 kilometres of railway and 300 kilometres of road were destroyed.

Tsunamis

If an earthquake or sudden volcanic eruption occurs near or beneath the sea, the jolt may be transferred to the sea in the form of a tsunami – a massive wave that sweeps across the ocean until it hits land. If the coast is heavily populated – and the vast majority of people in the world do live close to a coast – the loss of life can be huge. In 1755, Portugal's capital, Lisbon, was destroyed by an earthquake and the tsunami that followed half an hour later: thousands of people fleeing the earthquake (and consequent fires) mistakenly thought it was safer to stand on the shore. The tsunami that hit Indonesia, Thailand, Sri Lanka and India in December 2004 killed over 280,000 people. The tsunami was triggered by an undersea earthquake measuring 9.15 on the Richter scale. The force of the wave was so vast that it even killed people thousands of kilometres away on the east coast of Africa.

THE RESTLESS SKIES

The world's weather is equally turbulent, and can produce a range of natural disasters of colossal proportions. Tropical cyclones (also known as hurricanes in the Atlantic region or typhoons in the north-west Pacific region) are vicious storms, with winds of up to 320 kilometres per hour (kph) circulating in a diameter some 300 kilometres across around a calm central 'eye'. Tropical cyclones are caused by the warm climate around the Equator. Bangladesh has suffered the worst devastation from tropical cyclones, caused by the deadly combination of ferocious winds, high seas and heavy rains. It has been affected so badly because it is a low-lying country, which sits on a delta at sea level.

? Why are tsunamis so destructive?

Tsunamis are triggered by a massive disturbance in the sea, usually caused by an earthquake or a volcanic eruption, or sometimes by a landslide. The disturbance causes huge volumes of water to be displaced, and the surface of the sea wells up to form a vast, low wave. Out in mid-ocean, this may be barely noticeable, even though the wave can be moving at 800 kph. However, as the wave approaches the coast, and the sea becomes shallower, the friction between the moving water and the seabed causes the water to form a massive wave rising up from the sea. Some tsunamis rise to 100 metres high, but this is rare. Film footage of the 2004 tsunami hitting the coast of Thailand shows a relatively low wave, but the sheer volume and expanse of the wave were overwhelming. As the water hit the shoreline, it caused massive devastation to buildings and the loss of many lives.

When tropical cyclones hit the coast, they can throw boats out of harbours, tear through buildings, uproot trees, and rip down power and communication cables. Tropical cyclones are accompanied by heavy rainfall, and cause the sea to well up in 'storm surges' that can result in widespread flooding. In fact about 90 per cent of all deaths from tropical cyclones are caused by drowning. In 2005, flooding, caused by Hurricane Katrina, inundated the historic city of New Orleans, Louisiana, USA – a city largely built below sea level, almost surrounded by water and defended by embankments called levees that proved inadequate. Widespread damage was also inflicted along the coasts of Mississippi and Alabama.

Tornadoes

A tornado is another form of deadly wind. Caused by differences in atmospheric pressure and heat during thunderstorms, tornadoes form spiralling funnels of wind turning at speeds of up to 480 kph – powerful enough to pull off roofs and lift large trucks into the air. As they move across the landscape, tornadoes create relatively narrow paths of destruction. They can occur virtually anywhere in the world, including Britain, but the region most famous for its tornadoes is the USA. The 'Tornado Alley' of the American Midwest and South runs through most of the states from the Great Lakes in the north, to the Gulf of Mexico in the south. Texas, Oklahoma, Kansas and Nebraska regularly suffer ferocious tornadoes from March to October (the tornado season). In 1974, a record number of 144 tornadoes hit 13 US states over a period of just two days; 330 people died and 5,000 were injured. But the biggest death toll ever from a single tornado occurred in Bangladesh in 1989, when as many as 1,300 people died.

9

Tropical cyclones can be 300 kilometres wide and cause winds of up to 320 kph.

Tornadoes are powerful spiralling funnels of wind that travel over land at speeds of up to 480 km per hour.

FLOODING

Of all the weather-connected natural disasters, it is flooding that causes the most devastation and loss of life. Flooding is often the result of exceptional rainfall, which swells a river and can be combined with melting snow or storm surges from the sea. On average, floods cause more deaths each year than any other natural disaster. In Galveston, Texas, in the US, the hurricane-induced flood of September 1900 took at least 6,000 lives. In the Mississippi flood of 1993, only around 50 lives were lost, but damage was valued at US$20 billion. However, the world's worst floods have occurred in Bangladesh and China. In 1970, Bangladesh lost 500,000 lives and more than 130,000 more in 1991, from cyclone-induced flooding. The world's worst natural disaster in terms of human loss occurred in China in 1931, when the Huang He (Yellow River) flooded during heavy monsoon rains, and some three million people died from drowning, famine and disease.

10

Bangladesh: a special case

Bangladesh is a low-lying country riddled with the waterways formed by the huge delta of the River Brahmaputra, which flows out into the Bay of Bengal. Each year in summer, the river fills with the water from the melting snows of the Himalayas. But this is also the cyclone season, when strong winds, accompanied by heavy rains, bring flooding and storm surges from the sea. The many little islands of the delta are easily overwhelmed as river waters rise by up to two metres and the fragile homes of people who live there are severely damaged. Hundreds of thousands of lives have been lost in regular disasters in Bangladesh over the last century. Bangladesh is a poor country with a growing population; however, the incidence of disaster has been reduced in recent decades by improved flood defences and effective evacuation programmes.

Once a forest fire takes hold, it can burn for many weeks.

FIRE

A fire that gets out of control and becomes a natural disaster is often kick-started by the weather: long spells of sunny weather without rain can turn forests into huge areas of crisp and flammable material. It only takes a spark and a little wind to stir up a fire. Once a forest fire takes hold, it can create a front, many kilometres long, which at worst can move at 160 kph, with flames rising to 50 metres at scorching temperatures of 2,000°C. Such an event will destroy any building or living creature in its path. Forest fires are very hard to put out, and can burn for weeks. In October 2003, California's largest fire in recent history, the Cedar Fire in San Diego County, lasted for ten days, destroyed over 2,000 homes, killed 14 people and caused damage estimated at US$2 billion. There have also been particularly bad forest fires in recent years in southern France (2000/2005), Portugal (2003/2005) and southern Australia (2001–2002/2003).

Forest fires can be caused by a number of factors. Natural causes include lightning or volcanic lava. At other times, sunshine passing through discarded glass can ignite dry grass. But too often people are the cause, starting fires by carelessly lighting barbecues, throwing away cigarette ends, or even deliberately setting light to dry material.

The Spanish Flu

The most devastating epidemic in history occurred in 1918-19. This major outbreak of a worldwide disease (or 'pandemic') was caused by influenza (flu). Known as 'Spanish flu' or 'La Grippe' at the time, it is believed to have killed between 20 and 40 million people worldwide – more than were killed in the First World War.

Spanish flu was not like normal flu epidemics which have symptoms of a bad cold with fever. Instead, it caused headaches and delirium, and victims began coughing blood while their lungs filled with fluid. Some victims died within 48 hours of showing the first symptoms. Alarmingly, its effects were not confined to the very young and the elderly who are usually most at risk. Instead, it was just as likely to affect those who were young and healthy.

The epidemic lasted for eighteen months, then petered out. The exact cause remains unknown, but it was likely to have been a form of avian (bird) flu, called H1N1, that mutated (changed) so that it could be passed directly to humans, and then spread from human to human. Carried by soldiers and others on the move in the aftermath of the First World War, it infected just about all populations throughout the world.

ATTACKS ON HEALTH

Another way in which humans and nature can come into conflict is through the issue of disease. Disease is an inescapable feature of all forms of life. We all get ill, and many people become victims of fatal illnesses, such as cancer. Disease on an individual scale is not usually considered to be a natural disaster – devastating though it might be. But it can play a very destructive role in the aftermath of a natural disaster – such as cholera epidemics from drinking and washing in contaminated water. And any epidemic – affecting a widespread population, and having a direct impact on everyone – could also be thought of as a natural disaster.

11

Modern medicine has brought vaccinations against deadly diseases.

Can we fight the flu?

Influenza is a viral infection of the lungs that can cause fever, cough and severe muscle aches. Flu is particularly serious for the elderly and those who have respiratory conditions, such as asthma. But even the young and healthy can find flu debilitating for a few days.

Viral infections cannot be treated with antibiotics, but the onset of flu can be prevented with a flu vaccination. However, flu is difficult to treat because new strains of flu arise all the time and scientists have to continually create new vaccinations and anti-viral medicines. In 2003, an epidemic of bird flu swept through several countries in Asia, revealing a new strain of the virus known as H5. Although this strain is common among birds, it is not usually associated with humans. However, some people have become infected with H5N1 (a related flu that has an alarmingly high fatality rate). Scientists are watching closely to see if the virus changes into a form that can pass between humans. Dangerous H5 strains could be spread by migrating birds, and a global epidemic would require scientists to find an effective treatment fast.

Epidemics of the past

Today, epidemics are less common than they were in the past. This is largely due to improved hygiene standards and improved knowledge of disease prevention. The Black Death (1347-50) killed around one third of Europe's population (around 25 million people) and similar numbers in Asia and Africa. Once thought to have been a bubonic plague transmitted by rats, modern research suggests that other diseases may have been to blame, such as anthrax, or an Ebola-like disease (see page 13).

The Great Plague that hit England in 1665-66 was probably a bubonic plague, and killed around 100,000. In the 19th century, a series of pandemics (an epidemic on a global scale) spread the deadly water-borne disease cholera around the world, affecting India, China, Europe, North America and Africa and killing millions. The influenza pandemic of 1918-19 also killed between 20 and 40 million people worldwide (see page 11).

Today, international travel means that most people have been exposed to common diseases, and have a degree of immunity (natural defences) to them. But isolated communities may be vulnerable to diseases that are imported from abroad. This was the case in the Americas before the arrival of Europeans in the 16th century. The newcomers brought diseases that were common in Europe, such as measles, whooping cough and flu, but the Native Americans had no natural defences against them. In Central America and Mexico, the Native American population in 1500 was about 25 million. However, as a result of imported diseases (as well as war and slavery) their population was reduced to just 1.25 million by 1625.

The spread of disease

There have, in the past, been hopes of conquering disease, but some diseases have become a permanent battle against nature's destructive forces. New and dangerous diseases continue to emerge, such as Acquired Immune Deficiency Syndrome (AIDS), which was first identified in 1981 and has now killed more than 25 million people. This devastating disease destroys the body's natural ability to defend itself against infection. AIDS is caused by the Human Immunodeficiency Virus (HIV), which is transmitted by the exchange of infected body fluids, usually through sex, or, in the case of drug addicts, through the use of shared needles. A baby can also inherit the disease if their mother is infected. It is estimated that worldwide about 44 million people are now infected with HIV; some 3.5 million people died of the disease in 2004.

Another lethal disease is Ebola. First identified in 1976, this disease has a very high death rate, causing fever and a collapse of the internal organs and bleeding. It was feared that Ebola might turn into an international epidemic, but so far outbreaks have been limited to Africa; 224 people died from Ebola in Uganda in 2000-1.

Diseases that change

Meanwhile, old diseases change and adapt to defeat modern medicine. One of the worst of these is malaria, from which perhaps 515 million people are currently suffering, and which kills more than a million every year. Found mainly in the warmer parts of the world, malaria is caused by a parasite carried by female mosquitoes. Each time a new medicine is introduced to combat malaria, new strains emerge that resist the medicine. The same – if on a far smaller scale – goes for new infections found in hospitals, which have developed a resistance to antibiotics, such as MRSA (Methicillin-Resistant Staphylococcus Aureus) and C. difficile (Clostridium difficile), which infected 45,000 (mainly elderly) patients in Britain in 2004 and killed nearly 1,000 of them. Just as man thinks he is winning against nature in the battle against disease, nature fights back.

SARS

In 2002, a new pneumonia-like disease emerged called Severe Acute Respiratory Syndrome (SARS). The disease first appeared in China, but quickly spread to nearby countries, such as Hong Kong and Vietnam. Over 800 people were killed and the disease caused a major scare worldwide until it was brought under control a year later. The Chinese government initially tried to cover up the outbreak, which caused the disease to spread more rapidly. The country also suffered significant economic damage as workers were unwell and tourism decreased. Face masks were worn in China for some months.

DISASTER HOTSPOTS

We now know that some natural disasters are more likely to occur in particular places. This is largely due to tectonic plate activity and global weather patterns. This map outlines some of the major disaster hotspots around the world – from earthquakes and volcanoes to floods and famine.

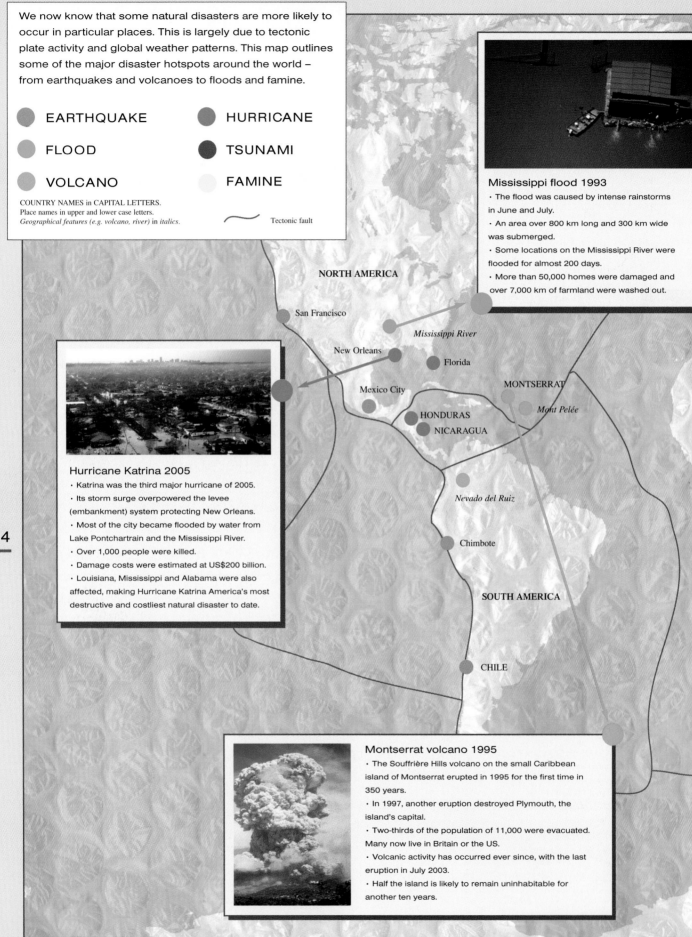

● EARTHQUAKE

● FLOOD

● VOLCANO

● HURRICANE

● TSUNAMI

● FAMINE

COUNTRY NAMES in CAPITAL LETTERS.
Place names in upper and lower case letters.
Geographical features (e.g. volcano, river) in italics.

〜 Tectonic fault

Mississippi flood 1993
· The flood was caused by intense rainstorms in June and July.
· An area over 800 km long and 300 km wide was submerged.
· Some locations on the Mississippi River were flooded for almost 200 days.
· More than 50,000 homes were damaged and over 7,000 km of farmland were washed out.

NORTH AMERICA

San Francisco

Mississippi River

New Orleans

Florida

Mexico City

MONTSERRAT

Mont Pelée

HONDURAS

NICARAGUA

Nevado del Ruiz

Chimbote

SOUTH AMERICA

CHILE

Hurricane Katrina 2005
· Katrina was the third major hurricane of 2005.
· Its storm surge overpowered the levee (embankment) system protecting New Orleans.
· Most of the city became flooded by water from Lake Pontchartrain and the Mississippi River.
· Over 1,000 people were killed.
· Damage costs were estimated at US$200 billion.
· Louisiana, Mississippi and Alabama were also affected, making Hurricane Katrina America's most destructive and costliest natural disaster to date.

14

Montserrat volcano 1995
· The Souffrière Hills volcano on the small Caribbean island of Montserrat erupted in 1995 for the first time in 350 years.
· In 1997, another eruption destroyed Plymouth, the island's capital.
· Two-thirds of the population of 11,000 were evacuated. Many now live in Britain or the US.
· Volcanic activity has occurred ever since, with the last eruption in July 2003.
· Half the island is likely to remain uninhabitable for another ten years.

DISASTER HOTSPOTS

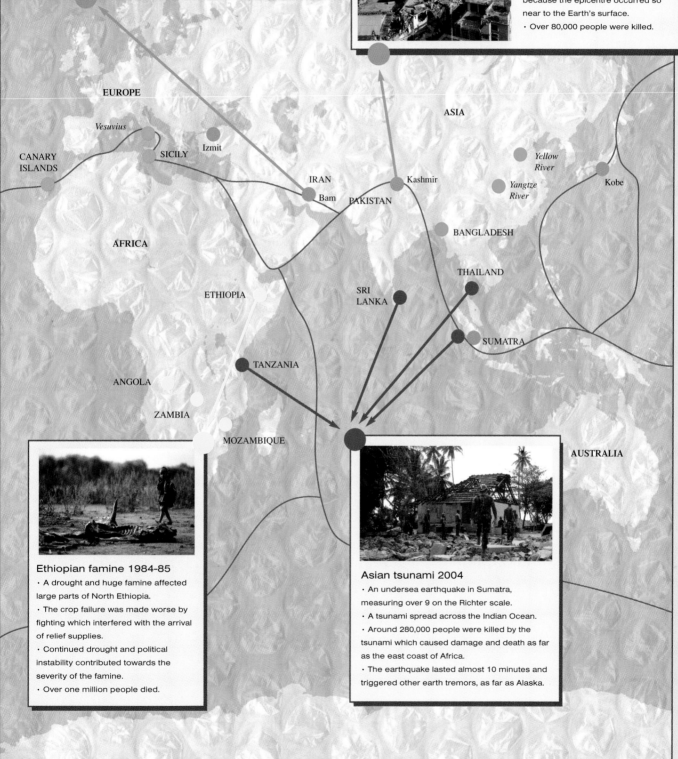

Bam earthquake 2003
- An earthquake measuring 6.5 on the Richter scale.
- Over 26,000 people were killed and 30,000 injured.
- 85 per cent of the city's buildings were destroyed.
- Around 75,000 people left homeless.

Pakistan earthquake 2005
- An earthquake measuring 7.6 on the Richter scale.
- The epicentre in Kashmir was worst affected.
- The earthquake was devastating because the epicentre occurred so near to the Earth's surface.
- Over 80,000 people were killed.

EUROPE

Vesuvius

CANARY ISLANDS

SICILY   Izmit

ASIA

Yellow River

Yangtze River

Kobe

IRAN
Bam   PAKISTAN   Kashmir

AFRICA

ETHIOPIA

BANGLADESH

THAILAND

SRI LANKA

ANGOLA

TANZANIA

SUMATRA

ZAMBIA

MOZAMBIQUE

AUSTRALIA

Ethiopian famine 1984-85
- A drought and huge famine affected large parts of North Ethiopia.
- The crop failure was made worse by fighting which interfered with the arrival of relief supplies.
- Continued drought and political instability contributed towards the severity of the famine.
- Over one million people died.

Asian tsunami 2004
- An undersea earthquake in Sumatra, measuring over 9 on the Richter scale.
- A tsunami spread across the Indian Ocean.
- Around 280,000 people were killed by the tsunami which caused damage and death as far as the east coast of Africa.
- The earthquake lasted almost 10 minutes and triggered other earth tremors, as far as Alaska.

ATTACKS ON FOOD

A natural disaster also occurs also when people's food supplies are dramatically affected by a natural cause – as a result of drought, for instance. If there has been no rain for a prolonged period of time and no alternative source of water is available, crops die in the fields and people run the risk of starvation.

In most places where drought is common, people have traditionally found ways of surviving – by depending on stores of food, or trading with neighbours, or using alternative water sources (such as irrigation systems or reservoirs). But such traditions can be undermined by war, refugee crises, problems with the distribution of food or by a large increase in population (perhaps because of better health).

Such factors put greater stress on an already delicate relationship with what nature can provide, and if the rains fail, a crisis will follow. This is what happened in the Horn of Africa (Ethiopia, Somalia) in the 1980s, when around one million people died. The worst recorded drought and famine was in China in 1876-9, when nine million people died.

Drought is a major cause of starvation and affects many parts of Africa and Asia.

Pests and diseases

Similarly, famine can occur when crops are attacked by disease, as happened in Ireland in 1845, when the potato crop was hit by a fungus. Pests, such as desert locusts, can also destroy crops. A vast swarm of locusts swept right across northern Africa in 2004, eating all the crops in their path. The United Nations' Food and Agriculture Organisation estimated that US$122 million was spent to fight the swarm, which nonetheless did US$2.5 billion worth of crop damage. Locusts have been a problem throughout history. They are mentioned in the Bible, referring to a plague that may have occurred in around 1300 BC.

In Niger, in 2005, the combined effects of a drought and a plague of locusts brought critical food shortages.

16

WHEN DISASTER STRIKES

Some natural disasters come with a warning, giving people time to avoid the worst. But others can strike suddenly, without warning at all. The most serious disasters cause multiple fatalities. Even those who survive need urgent aid as their homes and workplaces are destroyed and essential supplies such as water, electricity, roads and communication systems are affected. In the long term, the effects for the survivors of a disaster are just as serious, as they live with the memories for the rest of their lives.

In the aftermath of a disaster, the injured are the first priority.

The immediate aftermath

In the modern world, we are beginning to be able to predict the arrival of a natural disaster – a volcano may show increased activity or the beginnings of a hurricane can be spotted in a satellite image. But some disasters (especially earthquakes) can take us by surprise. In the short term, victims may suffer death or injury, the death of their loved ones, damage to their homes and workplaces, and disruption to local services. In the longer term, they may find that they cannot recover their health, their homes or their jobs, and their losses leave a deep mental scar that they must bear, possibly forever.

When a disaster strikes – during its moments, hours or days of impact – survival is the first priority for anyone caught up in the event. Natural disasters bring total chaos: victims will find their world collapsing around them. They may survive by quick thinking (sheltering in the strongest part of the house, or under a sturdy desk or table during an earthquake, for example) or simply by good fortune.

Rescue teams face a scene of chaos when they attend to a natural disaster.

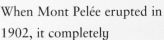

Picking up the pieces

When the event is over, the work begins. The first task for survivors is to try to find any other survivors who may be trapped and in need of rescue, but they may be too weakened or shocked themselves to do much. Surrounded by devastation, their homes destroyed, their loved ones missing, they may be too overwhelmed by panic, distress and bewilderment.

Fortunately, modern international communications mean that the world is quickly alerted to a natural disaster, and a plea for help usually results in rescue teams from other countries arriving on the scene very quickly. International organisations co-ordinate the relief effort and draw on specialist teams from around the world for the necessary requirements. Food supplies, medical equipment and experts such as doctors, nurses, firefighters, builders, engineers and electricians are all called upon to do what they can to minimise the impact of the disaster and to get people's lives back on track.

The aid effort is not without problems, however. Sometimes areas are very remote and difficult to access. At other times, the political situation in a country makes it very difficult for aid to get through to the people that need it most.

18

Misguided priorities

When Mont Pelée erupted in 1902, it completely destroyed the city of Saint-Pierre, capital of the French island of Martinique and the so-called 'Paris of the West Indies'; virtually the entire population of 36,000 people was killed. The volcano gave plenty of warnings about the imminent eruption, but the authorities delayed evacuation of the city because an election was about to be held.

On the morning of 8 May, a red cloud of ash covered the sky, then a huge explosion of burning gas heated to 815°C, filled the air beneath it and incinerated the town. Clocks stopped at 7.50am and melted. One of the three survivors was a prisoner awaiting trial, who was protected by the thick walls of his cell and dug out three days later; unable to contradict the judgement of God, the authorities released him.

Where possible, aid agencies try to reach the victims of a disaster as quickly as possible, with food and medical supplies.

Aid agencies are trained to assess and report the damage, and to alert all other teams that may be able to help. But their primary initial task is to find and rescue any survivors who are trapped, using heat-sensitive equipment, listening devices or sniffer dogs, and machinery to dig them out. Aid workers also have to organise emergency aid for the injured: death tolls may be high, but in any natural disaster there are likely to be far more people who are injured, many of them seriously. The survivors may need shelter, food, blankets and clothes.

The relief operation, if well run, has to make best use of all the available resources – the army, police, fire service, ambulance service, health professionals and first-aid experts, volunteers, transport methods (lorries, buses, helicopters and aeroplanes),

bulldozers to clear blocked roads and rubble, communication systems, shelter, medicine, food and financial donations. This is an immense task, and it has to be done very quickly: 90 per cent of earthquake victims die in the first 24 hours. Effective co-ordination is particularly difficult to achieve when the disaster covers a large area or a mountainous terrain. In the 2005 Kashmir earthquake, for example, many survivors in remote areas were left for months without adequate food, shelter and medical supplies.

The 2004 tsunami: can there even be too much aid?

On 26 December 2004, the world woke up to the news that a tsunami had struck the coast of Thailand. It soon became clear that a major disaster had occurred. Triggered by a powerful undersea earthquake to the west of Sumatra, the tsunami struck Thailand (killing around 11,000) but also wiped out coastal towns and villages in Aceh Province in Sumatra (causing at least 170,000 deaths). Meanwhile, another tsunami raced across the Indian Ocean causing devastation in India (16,000 deaths) and Sri Lanka (38,000 deaths). The total confirmed loss of life was 175,000 people, but the real figure probably exceeded 280,000. A colossal international rescue operation swung into action, assisted by huge donations given by governments and the public. News of the disaster spread around the world rapidly and

the presence of western tourists among the victims brought record donations from people in western nations. Shortly after the disaster, the health charity Médicins sans Frontières announced that it had actually received more donations that it could spend on tsunami relief, and asked donors to allow them to spend the excess money in other regions in need of aid. Nothing can measure the suffering of the survivors and the bereaved, and their suffering will continue for generations. But the hard truth is that far greater loss of life takes place all the time in forgotten parts of the world: 280,000 people die of AIDS and malaria every month in Africa, but they receive no such publicity or assistance.

19

A huge relief effort was needed to help the stranded survivors of Hurricane Katrina in 2005.

Days later

In the immediate aftermath of a disaster, it is essential to provide effective organisation, and law and order. Shock soon turns to desperation and anger if help does not arrive quickly, and desperate people will fight over relief supplies if they are not distributed in an orderly fashion. Imposing order may mean bringing in the army, and maybe even using guns to control looting and fighting.

As days pass, the chances of finding people alive amongst the wreckage and rubble diminish. But rescue teams have to keep on trying. Survivors have been found alive in collapsed buildings two weeks after an earthquake. Meanwhile, in situations where there has been widespread death and injury, there is a strong possibility of disease, especially if supplies of clean water have been interrupted and sanitation systems have broken down. When monsoon flooding hit Dhaka, the capital of Bangladesh, in 1988, it killed 5,000 people, made 21 million people homeless, and 160,000 people became infected with disease. Fears of a similar outbreak of

disease were raised in the aftermath of Hurricane Katrina in 2005, when New Orleans, USA, stood deep in water polluted by sewers, fuel and the bodies of dead people and animals.

Dealing with the dead can present a major problem. It may be impossible to bury the bodies quickly and safely. It may also be inappropriate to do so, for instance if bodies still need to be identified, or if they are foreigners, whose bodies need to be sent home. After the 2004 tsunami, thousands of bodies in Thailand were preserved in refrigeration containers and trucks for identification, a process that took many months.

Relief supplies need to be distributed in an orderly fashion to keep a disaster situation under control.

20

Another after-effect of a major disaster is the disruption to food supplies, and the complete destruction of crops and fields, threatening a food shortage not just for the immediate future but for several years. In the past, famine following a natural disaster may have killed more people than the natural disaster itself. For instance, when Mount Tambora erupted in 1815 on the island of Sumbaya in Indonesia, 12,000 died on the island itself (only 26 of its inhabitants survived), but a further 80,000 died in the famine that followed in neighbouring islands, because the vast quantities of ash discharged from the volcano wrecked the farmland and fishing grounds. Today, however, international agencies can usually bring food supplies quickly by plane and ship, and endeavour to continue to do so until the victims have recovered. That said, sometimes the international community is slow to react to aid agency warnings about a crisis. The famine in Niger in 2005, for example, reached catastrophic proportions before adequate help arrived.

Missing persons

In a major disaster, such as an earthquake in a city, or a tsunami, some people simply disappear. They vanish beneath the rubble of a towerblock, melt into crowds fleeing in panic, or are swept away by the waves. No one knows if they are alive or dead. The families of the missing desperately search hospitals, first-aid tents and mortuaries where the dead lie. They put pictures of their missing loved ones on notice boards in the hope that someone will recognise them. Often, babies and infants who become separated from their families cannot be identified, especially if their parents have died. Such problems become even more

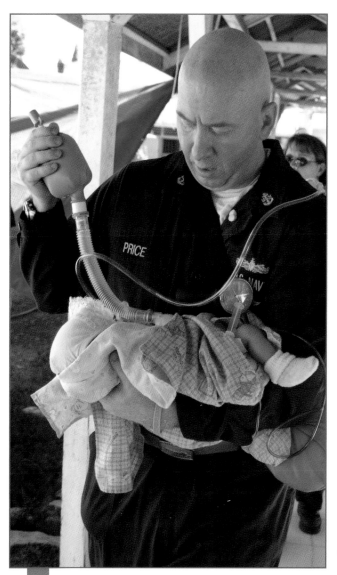

Military personnel can provide vital emergency aid. Here, a member of the US navy gives medical assistance to a baby caught up in an earthquake in Indonesia.

21

difficult when refugees from a disaster are spread over a large area – perhaps bussed out of the disaster zone to towns and cities some distance away. It is possible also that all communication systems (where they exist) will have collapsed, such as telephone cables and mobile-phone masts. Happy stories will emerge when the missing are found and reunited with their families; but there are always tragic tales when people discover that their loved ones have not survived. And the fate of the missing may never be known.

Rich and poor

Disasters affect people in different ways. In richer countries, houses are stronger, there are more hospitals, better emergency services, better disaster planning programmes and better communication systems. The media (notably the television services) ensure that everyone becomes immediately aware of a crisis and encourage them to respond with help or donations. Advanced transport systems also mean that the injured can be evacuated and supplies can be brought in. In contrast, poorer countries do not have the people, equipment, services and supplies to help in quite the same way. Instead, they depend on international help in the time of a disaster. But rich countries can also be caught unprepared. Hurricane Katrina was probably America's worst natural disaster. It showed that even the USA – the world's wealthiest nation – was unable to respond quickly and adequately to such a disaster.

Hurricane Katrina: an avoidable disaster

Hurricane Katrina struck the southern coast of the USA with terrifying force in September 2005. A storm surge caused the sea to overwhelm the flood defences of the city of New Orleans. Hundreds died as the city was flooded, and nearly half a million people had to abandon their homes. The national and state governments soon came under criticism for their slow reaction to the crisis, and the fact that warnings of this widely predicted disaster had not been heeded.

At the time, a full emergency plan had been devised, but the Federal Emergency Management Agency (FEMA) failed to act upon it: it was known, for example that at least 100,000 people – the poor, the aged and the sick – would need assistance in evacuating. Instead, no significant help arrived in the city until four days after the disaster.

Now the USA faces a bill of at least $200 billion, as well as the prospect of long-term hardship for hundreds of thousands of people. In the event, it was the poor again who suffered the most. Many could not flee the city to safety because they did not have cars, or even the money to pay for a bus fare – or anywhere to go if they did.

REBUILDING LIVES

Humans are very adaptable: we have suffered from natural disasters throughout our history and survived. Archaeological evidence of disasters that occurred in history can be found all over the world. And just as disasters have happened in the past, they will continue to happen in the future. Disasters strike, people suffer the effects, and then they rebuild their lives and learn valuable lessons. But no one who has ever experienced a natural disaster will be untouched: their view of the world will have changed forever.

Hurricane Mitch
In October and November 1998, Hurricane Mitch, one of the most destructive hurricanes on record, tore through Central America, unleashing torrents of rainwater that turned city streets into lethal rivers. Towns, roads and bridges were destroyed by mudslides, crops were wiped out, and 18,000 people were killed – one of the highest-ever death tolls for a hurricane – as the path of the storm crossed Nicaragua and headed into Honduras, then El Salvador and Guatemala. It takes huge investment over a long period to rebuild roads and to get communication systems up and running again. Much of the destruction wiped out valuable farmland, such as banana plantations, which have been ruined. This part of Central America has still not recovered form Hurricane Mitch.

Recovery
Standing amid the ruins of a town – wrecked by a hurricane, an earthquake or a tsunami – anyone must wonder just how it can be built again. After the emergency workers have gone home, after the dead have been buried, and the injured have been taken care of, this is the prospect that faces the survivors. An immense task lies ahead. It is not simply a question of rebuilding, and of reconstructing all the complex systems on which a town depends – electricity, running water, drains, communication systems, roads, transport. None of this will happen unless the people who come back to live in the town can recover their livelihoods. They need jobs and they need shops, healthcare, and schools for their children. The entire, complex system of urban life has to be rebuilt and re-equipped. There may be serious obstacles to achieving this. For instance, the economic base of the town may have been destroyed by the disaster – factories, or beaches and hotels that formerly attracted tourists – making it impossible for people to earn a living again.

Another obstacle is that there may simply not be enough people left. Natural disasters can cause major changes to a population. Many people may have died, but even more are likely to be refugees who never go back to their ruined towns and cities: they may be unable, or just unwilling, to return home.

Hidden damage

Natural disasters can also have a profound psychological impact. Many victims will suffer mentally from the shock of the traumatic event that they have witnessed, and may have 'post traumatic stress disorder', causing nightmares or permanent anxiety. People will have lost loved ones, and may even have seen them dying. Many will have lost all their possessions – including all the things that link them to their past, such as family photos, books and personal records, such as bank statements or their passport and driving licence. They also may have lost their jobs. In other words, many survivors lose almost everything that reminded them of who they were; they lose their identity. Some people will be able to cope with this, but others will never recover, and will be traumatised for the rest of their lives. Survivors may get help from the authorities; some will see professional counsellors who are trained to help people through psychological trauma; some may get compensation payments. Religious groups may also be able comfort survivors – although some victims may find that the natural disaster has destroyed the basis of any religious beliefs that they might have had.

Montserrat

Previously thought dormant, the volcano called Soufrière Hills on Montserrat began to erupt in 1995, and in 1997 it destroyed the capital, Plymouth. The British government – which is responsible for this small Caribbean island – felt it had no option: for the safety of the people in the path of the volcano, it ordered an evacuation, and two-thirds of the population of 11,000 left, most going to Britain, where they have since been granted full citizenship. The volcanic activity has diminished, but half the island is likely to remain uninhabitable for another ten years. The remainder is now considered safe to live in and some 300 Montserratians that went to the USA are now under pressure to leave, or be deported. But there is little to do on the island, with the old capital in ruins, little economic activity of any kind, and the tourist industry only just beginning to recover (a new airport opened in 2005). Many Montserratians want to return home, but the future on their island looks very uncertain.

Emergency aid is the first step in recovery,
but after a disaster like the Asian tsunami, many
victims have to rebuild their lives from scratch.

A plan for recovery

A key to the success of any plan for recovery is the ability to organise the work effectively – to bring order to a situation of utter chaos, and to target clear goals. Effective governments can mobilise the workforce and resources, and appoint officials to oversee the work. Aid and funding for reconstruction may be available through the United Nations and various international aid agencies, and these organisations have experts who are trained to offer advice based on wide experience of other disasters. Some funding may also come from insurance policies taken out by individuals, businesses and organisations to compensate for losses when disasters occur.

In the immediate aftermath of a natural disaster, there is usually plenty of goodwill from fellow citizens and from abroad. But more difficult times lie ahead, after several months or years, when the world has turned its attention elsewhere. Recovery is a long and slow process. Political groups will re-emerge and start arguing about what is being done – whether those in power are doing enough for the victims, and whether aid money is being usefully spent. The goodwill and generosity that came immediately after the disaster can quickly become the source of squabbles, resentment and accusations of corruption. Following the 2004 tsunami in Sri Lanka, for instance, there were complaints that local officials were distributing aid mainly to their supporters, some of whom were not even victims of the tsunami; the government was accused of giving priority and financial help to the tourist trade, to rebuild hotels and other facilities, at the expense of local fishermen.

Religious groups may also create divisions. There will always be religious groups who claim that a natural disaster is a sign from God, sent to punish the victims for their wickedness. This has been the case in the past: the 1906 earthquake in San Francisco was the first major natural disaster which was not viewed by the majority as some kind of punishment from God. But similar religious voices were still heard after the Asian tsunami in 2004, and Hurricane Katrina and the earthquake in Pakistan in 2005.

An Iranian government official visits patients at the US field hospital after the Bam earthquake of 2003.

PROBLEMS WITH AID

Natural disasters can inspire great public sympathy: donations by private individuals to relief funds can shame governments into being more generous. But donations by both governments and individuals are often uneven.

The amount of aid that is given to a country in the time of disaster often relates to the relationship between countries during normal times. Donors are likely to be more generous to countries that they sympathise with, or that are allies. After the Bam earthquake in Iran in 2003, which killed over 26,000 people and injured perhaps 30,000 more, US$1.1 billion of aid was pledged – but a year later only US$17.5 million had been received, according to Iranian government sources. This may be partly due to the uneasy relationship that Iran has with the western world in quite different fields, such as its history of anti-Americanism, and its nuclear development programme. Such political issues can reduce significantly the aid given by donor nations.

Aid, too, can cause its own problems. Aid agencies have learnt that they cannot simply move in, give help over a short period following a crisis, and then move out. This can shatter the local economy, already made fragile by the disaster. If clothes, medicines, tents and blankets are provided free, and without careful analysis of local emergency needs, local merchants, who make a living by selling these items, are likely to find their livelihoods wrecked in the long term. Feeding camps, where drought victims are sheltered and fed for free, can cause long-term damage to farming and village life. Aid is not just a question of generosity: it has to be delivered carefully.

LEARNING THE LESSONS

Some areas hit by natural disasters never fully recover. Galveston was Texas's largest and most prosperous city before it was hit by the devastating hurricane of 1900; after that, Houston grew at Galveston's expense. The town of Armero in Colombia, buried by the mudslide from the

Nevado del Ruiz volcano in 1985, has remained buried. But other areas hit by disaster can recover quickly – and usually more quickly in wealthy countries than in the poorer countries, for obvious reasons. The city of Kobe in Japan, for example, was hit by an earthquake in 1995, but has now been completely rebuilt.

Before long, the raw memories of a disaster may fade, and soon it may seem – almost – as though it never happened. With luck, though, the victims will not have entirely forgotten it, so that they can be better prepared the next time a disaster occurs. But there is no guarantee that they will be so wise. All too often, people put memories of a disaster aside, and start believing that it will never happen again.

Construction workers begin rebuilding this village school in Sri Lanka after the Asian tsunami of 2004.

Can we find positives in a natural disaster?

Some natural phenomena associated with natural disasters bring major benefits – which is why large populations often develop precisely where disaster might strike. For instance, volcanic soil is very fertile, so the slopes of volcanoes such as Villarica in Pucon, Chile (below) and volcanic islands are often heavily populated by farming communities.

River flooding can spread rich silt over the river valley, fertilising the farmland. The regular flooding of the River Nile in Egypt and the Yangtze River in China created highly productive farmlands that led to the development of two of the world's first civilisations. But river flooding also poses a threat to the large populations that live in these river valleys. The River Nile is now controlled by the Aswan High Dam, and the Yangtze River will soon be controlled by the huge new Three Gorges Dam.

Some ecologies (for example, grasslands and dry scrubland) actually need occasional fires to preserve the mix of plants and to control the growth of aggressive, untypical plants. Some seeds will in fact only germinate after a fire.

The impact of a natural disaster on human populations can – after the initial suffering – bring about change and renewal and encourage a fresh start. For example, the city of Dubrovnik, in Croatia, was destroyed in an earthquake in 1667, but it was rebuilt to become one of the finest Baroque cities in Europe.

27

PLANNING AHEAD

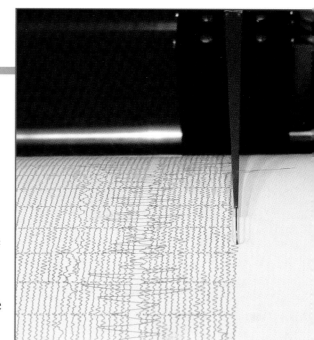

Because we know that some natural disasters follow patterns, it should be possible to take action to reduce the amount of death, damage and destruction of some disasters in the future. We can study the natural phenomena that cause disasters, set up equipment to look for warnings and change building techniques to withstand the threat. We can also arrange procedures for evacuation, teach people about survival techniques and plan emergency responses. Increasingly, people around the world expect their governments to provide some level of protection against predictable natural disasters.

This seismograph is used to monitor Earth tremors that might cause an earthquake.

MONITORING AND WARNING

If natural disasters were entirely predictable they would not be nearly so destructive. People would prepare and evacuate in time. But unfortunately, many natural disasters take us by surprise.

It is possible to track hurricanes as they make their way across the Atlantic Ocean, and to calculate their destructive power. But it is impossible to predict exactly what path they will take. Nonetheless, we know enough to broadcast warnings on radio and television to people who may be in danger. Americans are used to acting upon hurricane warnings: they close their storm shutters, board up their windows, fix down anything that can move, and – in extreme cases – evacuate in plenty of time.

Hurricane watch

Hurricanes usually begin in the eastern Atlantic, close to Africa, or in the Caribbean Sea. Early signs of a hurricane can be detected by satellite. When the winds reach 62 kph they are designated as tropical storms and given a name (in alphabetical order, alternating between male and female names); when they reach 117 kph, they are called hurricanes. The eye of a hurricane moves relatively slowly. Its track can be monitored by satellite and the specially equipped aircraft of the US National Hurricane Center. A hurricane's force and direction can be predicted with some accuracy: warnings are sent out to the region most likely to be hit, so that people can secure their properties, find shelter or evacuate the area.

The ones to watch

Several of the world's volcanoes are causing concern, and threaten a major disaster:

• Vesuvius, Naples, Italy. Famous for the destruction of Pompeii in AD79, Mount Vesuvius has erupted in cycles of activity. It last erupted in 1944. Many believe that its next eruption is imminent, and Naples – a city of 1.1 million people – lies beneath it.

• Popocatépetl, Mexico. The last major eruption was in 1947, and the volcano has recently been showing increased activity; in 2000, nearby towns had to be evacuated for a time. The city of Puebla (population 4.4 million) is 40 km away.

• Cumbre Vieja, La Palma, Canary Islands (below). Some believe that this unstable volcanic ridge threatens to cause a landslide, tipping 500 km^3 of soil into the sea. This could trigger a mega-tsunami that would hit the coasts of Africa, Europe and eastern North America within hours.

Predicting a volcanic eruption

Monitoring stations on active volcanoes listen out for any movement (seismic activity) that might indicate that an eruption is beginning, and watch for any changes in the volume of gases that emerge from the vents. Satellites are also used to help gather information from the sensors installed on volcanoes. Scientists studying a volcano ('volcanologists') and the local authorities will have devised careful plans for action at each sign of increased volcanic activity, leading up to complete evacuation of any area that might be in the blast zone of the volcano.

Equipment monitoring earthquakes at sea can issue warnings about a tsunami; if broadcast quickly enough, people on the coasts may have time to retreat to higher ground. A tsunami warning system will soon be installed in the Indian Ocean to prevent another tragedy like the one that occurred in 2004 (see page 8). Some experts argued that this should have been done before, but in fact tsunamis are rare in the region – the last major one occurred in 1883, when a volcano destroyed the island of Krakatau in Indonesia. All too often, precautions are only taken after a major natural disaster has occurred (such as building new earthquake-proof buildings or installing prediction equipment). Earthquakes on land are the most unpredictable of all natural disasters. Increased seismic activity may give some warning, but most occur out of the blue, to devastating effect.

MINIMISING THE IMPACT

But even earthquake zones are not helpless. Public advice programmes can teach people living there how to improve their chances of surviving a major earthquake. Modern building regulations should ensure that all new buildings in such an area (particularly public buildings, such as schools and hospitals) are designed to withstand an earthquake, for example, by incorporating steel supports that will stop ceilings from collapsing. If more buildings had been earthquake-proof in Pakistan, many deaths from the 2005 earthquake could have been prevented.

Education plays an important part in minimising the impact of a natural disaster. An example emerged after the 2004 tsunami in the Indian Ocean. When the sea drew back unusually far from the coast, some people knew this was a sign of an incoming tsunami – including a 10-year-old British girl who encouraged others to flee the coast. Most people did not know this, however, and some wandered onto the exposed beach in curiosity. Precisely the same thing happened during the earthquake and tsunami that destroyed Lisbon in 1755. In future, if all people living in these disaster areas are equipped with better knowledge and understanding, many lives could be saved. The United Nations has a department called the International Strategy for Disaster Reduction (UNISDR). It collects and spreads information about how the impact of disasters can be reduced by practical measures, such as assessing the risk of future disasters, installing warning mechanisms, applying improved building techniques and promoting education to prepare people for when disaster strikes.

Emergency planning

Local authorities take measures that are appropriate to the particular threats that their community faces. For example, in areas that are vulnerable to hurricanes, tropical storms or tornadoes, local authorities can protect their citizens by building public storm shelters and installing tornado sirens. Many Caribbean islands have hurricane shelters, built of concrete and steel, where islanders can go

Disaster-proof buildings

When San Francisco was hit by an earthquake in 1906, the houses – which were largely made of wood – stood up fairly well. But the resulting fires, caused by overturned stoves and burst gas pipes, destroyed the city. The lesson here was that buildings with some kind of structural flexibility can survive earthquakes. Modern buildings in earthquake zones – in the USA and Japan, for example – are designed with a variety of mechanisms to survive earthquakes, such as massive steel structures, flexible joints, and dampers or shock-absorbers in the foundations (rather like the shock-absorbers in a car). However, in the poorer areas of the world, where houses are often built cheaply and badly, large numbers of deaths occur during earthquakes.

The 'disaster movie' called *Twister* (1996) tells the story of a group of 'storm chasers' who take incredible risks to monitor tornadoes in the USA. It also features tornado shelters – the means by which a lot of families in the Midwest, and especially in northern Texas and Oklahoma, protect themselves from tornadoes (below). Modern tornado shelters are small concrete bunkers built into the home or dug into the garden, and covered with a heavy steel lid. This lid, which also serves as the door, has to be able to withstand upward wind forces that are quite capable of lifting entire buildings high into the air.

The initial tsunami waves caused by the undersea earthquake off the island of Sumatra in Indonesia on 26 December 2004, took just over two hours to reach the coast of Sri Lanka. This NASA satellite image shows deep ocean tsunami waves about 30-40 km from Sri Lanka's southwestern coast.

when a hurricane is predicted. Some towns in the USA have similar large concrete shelters specially built to protect their citizens against tornadoes, and have tornado sirens to give warnings when a tornado threatens.

Getting people to safety needs planning, organisation and discipline. Warnings for evacuation have to be issued in good time, and people have to know what they are meant to do and where to go. This requires education and practice. Bangladesh has been the scene of some

of the worst natural disasters in history, caused by tropical cyclones. In recent years, evacuation schemes, put into operation in the face of incoming storms, as well as hundreds of specially built cyclone shelters and flood-proof buildings, have succeeded in saving countless lives; during a major tropical cyclone in 1997, for example, some 500,000 people were saved by emergency measures, and only 67 died.

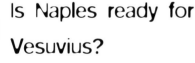

Is Naples ready for Vesuvius?

The city of Naples and the neighbouring towns that lie at the foot of Mount Vesuvius acknowledge that this volcano will, one day, erupt again. Vesuvius is the kind of volcano that will produce vast quantities of ash and large lumps of rocky debris that will fall on the surrounding towns, damaging buildings, injuring people and blocking roads. It may also produce lethal clouds of burning gas. The effect on the towns will depend on wind direction, but at least 500,000 people live in the danger zone, if not three million. Scientists are monitoring the volcanic activity and evacuation plans are in place. However, this will not be easy. How do the authorities warn people without causing panic? What do they do about

people who refuse to leave? What happens to those who do not have their own cars? Can the public transport systems cope with increased demand? Where will 500,000 people go? Temporary shelter, and food, would have to be provided for those who could not stay with friends or family outside the danger zone. Such a situation will seem justified if the eruption then actually takes place. But what should the authorities do if volcanic activity continues, without an eruption, for months? Should the evacuees be allowed back, to try to resume their lives, their jobs, their schooling?

Preventative measures

Governments and local authorities also have to undertake the kind of building work needed to defend communities against danger – such as dykes to protect land from flooding and firebreaks to limit the spread of forest fires. Likewise, they have to train the emergency services to cope with disasters, and set up specialist departments to co-ordinate national and international help when a disaster occurs. As Hurricane Katrina proved, it is best if this work is done at a local as well as a national level. When disasters strike, local people are more effective at bringing help quickly; government help takes longer to arrive, and foreign help takes even longer.

Controlling disease

Similar strategies also apply to disease, particularly diseases that can spread in the aftermath of a disaster. The first priority must be prevention. Clean water supplies and adequate sanitation need to be provided to prevent the risk of disease spreading. The injured need to be taken to medical facilities (which may just be make-shift hospital tents) where they can be cared for. The dead also need to be dealt with. Refrigeration containers are often used if bodies still need to be identified, but public health comes first: if bodies need to be disposed of quickly for the safety of others, the authorities will do so.

The risk of a worldwide epidemic, or pandemic, can be reduced by medical research and careful monitoring to identify the first warning signs. A vaccination programme can also be used as a preventative measure for those most vulnerable. Governments need to have stocks of any appropriate vaccine at the ready, or be able to produce them fast.

Education plays a vital role in disease control. Simple hygiene (such as hand-washing) can prevent the spread of disease, as well as an understanding about the importance of clean water, and how to make water pure for consumption. Ignorance is one of the main causes of the rapid spread of disease: education and public awareness campaigns can teach people how to maximise their chances of keeping healthy. And if the public are informed they can help governments by reducing the risk of an epidemic spreading to unmanageable proportions.

Health education is vital if populations are to minimise their risk of catching deadly diseases.

When an epidemic does occur, nations have to be ready to fight it. This may mean calling in international experts, isolating the victims and closing down travel routes (such as airlines and airports) through which infection might be spread. Above all, governments have to be open and honest about epidemic diseases: any attempt to hide an outbreak (for instance in order to protect businesses or tourism) can be disastrous, as China found in the SARS outbreak in 2002–3 (see page 13).

Polio makes a comeback

The year 2005 was supposed to mark the time when the World Health Organisation could announce the complete eradication of polio. This dangerous infectious disease, which causes infant paralysis, especially in the legs, has been the target of a worldwide immunisation programme over the last 50 years. Unfortunately, polio has recently made a comeback in Africa and now in Yemen and Indonesia. The re-emergence of polio began in 2003 in West Africa, where Islamic leaders discouraged immunisation, suspecting that it might be part of a US plot against Islam. While immunisation was suspended for 10 months, polio spread in Nigeria and to 10 other African countries.

Hospitals are well equipped to care for the sick, but could they cope with a pandemic?

CALCULATING THE COST

It is impossible for any government to be totally prepared for a natural disaster. If, for example, bird flu broke out in Britain, millions of people might catch it. Medical authorities can stockpile vaccines to protect people from the disease, and anti-viral drugs to treat those who catch it, but neither are guaranteed to work, because new strains of this dangerous flu emerge all the time. If a major flu epidemic occurred, hospitals would be quickly overwhelmed by the demand for beds.

Planners have to balance the risk of an event occurring against the immense cost of preparing for something that may not happen. When it comes to planning ahead, it is easier for the wealthy countries of the world to make the necessary investment than it is for poorer countries that are already struggling to provide basic day-to-day services for their citizens. Most nations that suffer from earthquakes cannot afford to have a fleet of rescue helicopters simply waiting for the next disaster to happen. We have come a long way in learning about how we can try to predict the effects of natural disasters, but because it is so unpredictable, nature will always have the upper hand.

33

Man's Effect on Nature

As the dominant species of planet Earth, humans have a growing population which is ever more greedy for food and products. In recent decades the alarming effect of man on nature has become clear. As we trawl the oceans for fish to eat, and tear down the forests for timber and farmland, we also pollute the natural world. Nature has the

power to unleash natural disasters, but it also has a delicate side that depends on fragile balances. These fragile balances can be upset by man's careless behaviour, with catastrophic consequences. While we're doing much to avoid disasters, we are also doing other things that actually encourage disasters to happen.

MISMANAGING NATURE

The deserts of the world are expanding. To some degree, this is a natural process: cave paintings in the middle of the Sahara desert indicate that in prehistoric times, the region was not a desert at all. But man's behaviour is accelerating this process: by using too much water, chopping down trees for firewood, and overgrazing the sparse pasture. This process is risking the livelihoods of the farmers who make their living on the edges of the desert.

Sand storms are now a common occurrence in areas where deserts are encroaching on neighbouring farmland.

The mismanagement of land is nothing new. From the late 19th century, the prairie grasslands of the American Midwest were ploughed up to grow grain. When there was a drought in the 1930s, the dry topsoil turned to a choking dust that was blown about in the wind, and vast areas of land became an unusable 'Dust Bowl'. Thousands died of starvation and lung diseases caused by the dust, and 350,000 had to leave their land and move elsewhere. A similar process is currently under way in the Amazon rainforest of Brazil, where trees are torn down to make farmland, which quickly becomes exhausted and useless for growing crops. In an effort to redress the balance, many initiatives are now being set up to regenerate farmland in desert areas and to replant forested areas.

When forests in hills and mountains are cut down, the exposed soil cannot absorb the rain. This causes flooding as the rainwater rushes off the hillsides and into the rivers. Bangladesh, for example, is affected by repeated flooding caused by rainwater originating in the Himalayas. Dams and levees have been set up to reduce the risk of flooding, but water needs to be carefully managed. In the USA, for example, the system of levees designed to prevent flooding from the Mississippi River was actually thought to contribute to severe flooding in the region in 1993, by interfering with the natural flow of the river.

The Aral Sea disaster

The Aral Sea, bordering Kazakhstan and Uzbekistan, was once a large, healthy, mildly salty inland sea of 26,000 km², where fleets of fishing boats caught 44,000 tonnes of fish a year. But during the 1960s, the Soviet government began diverting water from the rivers feeding the Aral Sea to irrigate the region's vast fields growing 'white gold' – cotton. As a result, the sea shrank to just 9,000 km², leaving coastal towns miles from the water's edge, and their ships stuck in dry mud. Worse, the water became intensely salty, killing the fish, while areas of dried seabed created salt-laden dust storms that wrecked the surrounding agricultural land. The fate of the Aral Sea represents one of the worst ecological disasters caused directly by the misguided action of man. Irrigation schemes are now being considered to help save the sea.

 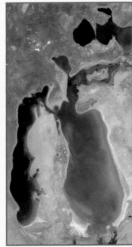

1989   2003

35

In 1993, the Mississippi and Missouri Rivers in the USA flooded after months of heavy rain. Fifty people died, 70,000 people were made homeless and vast areas of farmland became temporarily unusable. Here the floodwater has invaded Jefferson City, Missouri.

Nature as a dustbin

Meanwhile, man carelessly pollutes nature with waste products. Industrial waste poured into rivers destroys the life forms in the rivers, and makes the water unusable for consumption. Rain that falls on fields that have been enriched by chemical fertilisers can end up in rivers and then in the sea, creating a 'red bloom' of algae that poisons fish and destroys coral reefs. Virtually all life in the water off the coast of Shanghai in China has been destroyed by pollution in the Yangtze River. A similar 'dead zone' occurs each summer off the coast of Louisiana, USA.

Destructive gases

Gases released into the air, such as chlorine and bromine, damage the ozone layer in the atmosphere, which protects life on Earth from the Sun's powerful rays that can cause skin cancer. Large holes in the ozone layer (see box) have been detected over the Antarctic, affecting the ozone layer as far north as

Australia. But fossil fuels (coal, oil and gas) are causing the most concern. Every day, the burning of fossil fuels – to run power stations, factories, aeroplanes and cars – releases vast quantities of carbon dioxide (CO_2) and other gases into the air, which scientists think is causing 'global warming'. The search for alternative forms of energy, such as wind and solar power, to reduce this impact, is now more important than ever.

Industrial waste pollutes natural water sources, endangering river life and making the water unsafe to drink.

Is global warming really happening?

'Global warming' is a term that describes an increase in the average temperature of the Earth's atmosphere that can cause climate change. Average global temperatures have risen by 0.6°C since 1900, and the speed of increase seems to be accelerating. Some predictions suggest that by the year 2100, average global temperatures could have risen by 5.8°C.

One major effect of these rising temperatures would be the melting of polar ice caps, releasing billions of cubic kilometres of water into the sea. In 2005, US scientists discovered that the Arctic ice cap has already shrunk

significantly. Scientists also believe that global warming will lead to a weaker ozone layer (right). However, the precise effects of global warming are very hard to predict. For instance, as the polar ice caps melt, they might force cold water to travel around the oceans, causing temperatures in Europe to actually become colder.

Global warming could be part of a natural cycle of warming and cooling that the Earth goes through over time. But more and more scientists are now convinced that human activity is responsible: by burning fossil fuels, humans are creating a layer of pollution in the atmosphere that prevents some of the Sun's rays from escaping. Governments cannot afford to gamble on whether this theory is true or not: if they wait for proof it may be too late to do anything about it.

Already global warming is being linked to some natural disasters. As sea levels rise with the melting of the polar ice caps, nations around the world are reporting higher tides and greater risks of flooding; sea levels have already risen by 15 centimetres in the last ten years. Some predictions suggest that if world temperatures rise by 5°C by 2100, the sea will rise by one metre, swamping many low-lying islands and coasts.

Many of the port cities around the world are under increased threat from flooding: in London, the Thames Barrier, designed to protect the city from exceptionally high tides, may prove inadequate, and there is already talk of building a much larger barrier further downstream across the Thames Estuary. There is also a remote possibility that the vast West Antarctic ice sheet might one day collapse, releasing 3.2 million cubic kilometres of ice into the oceans and raising sea levels by five metres – enough to inundate virtually all coastal cities around the world.

If ice caps continue to melt, we are in danger of serious flooding.

The Thames Barrier protects London from high tides, but is it big enough?

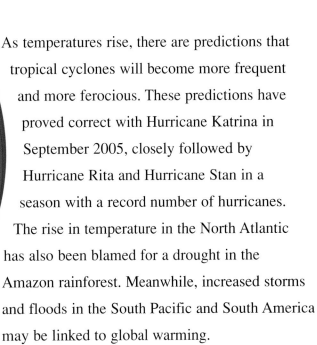

37

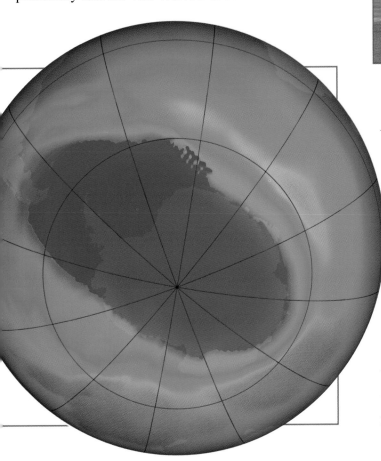

As temperatures rise, there are predictions that tropical cyclones will become more frequent and more ferocious. These predictions have proved correct with Hurricane Katrina in September 2005, closely followed by Hurricane Rita and Hurricane Stan in a season with a record number of hurricanes.

The rise in temperature in the North Atlantic has also been blamed for a drought in the Amazon rainforest. Meanwhile, increased storms and floods in the South Pacific and South America may be linked to global warming.

Encouraging disease

Human activity can also stimulate disease and trigger epidemics. The danger of bird flu has increased because we keep thousands of chickens, and other domestic birds, in close confinement in battery farms. Today, people also travel frequently around the globe, so a new outbreak of bird flu causes great concern. Any deadly new strain of bird flu could quickly be carried around the planet by tourists and business travellers within hours.

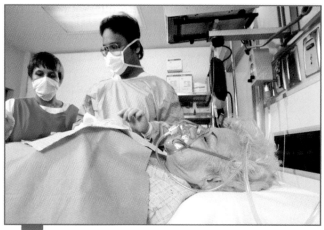

Modern medicine has made great advances, but new dangers are posed by human behaviour and misguided practices.

Messing around with nature can have serious consequences. The cattle brain disease called Bovine Spongiform Encephalopathy (BSE, also known as 'Mad Cow Disease') was probably caused by farmers feeding animal-based products (ground-up meat and bone-meal) to cattle – which are naturally vegetarian – in order to promote their growth. BSE is believed to be the cause of variant Creutzfeldt-Jacobs Disease (CJD), a fatal and incurable brain disease in humans. During the

1990s, it was widely feared that the infection of humans from BSE-contaminated beef was so widespread that an epidemic of CJD would follow, killing tens of thousands of people. It is a prediction that fortunately has (so far) not come true, but at the cost of slaughtering more than a million cattle to stop the spread of BSE. The most cases of BSE were found in England, but cattle in Europe, Japan and America were also affected.

NEW THREATS

Man may be taking risks with nature in other ways. Genetic modification – altering the gene structure – to improve crop yields may have unpredictable consequences, which is why the European Union (EU) insists on lengthy and detailed tests before genetically modified (GM) crops are adopted.

Meanwhile, arms manufacturers around the world – governments as well as terrorists – experiment with biological weapons designed to spread diseases (such as anthrax, Ebola, smallpox or the bubonic plague) that might cause an epidemic among their enemies. Any use of these, or even an accident, could have disastrous consequences.

The US military forces used chemicals such as Agent Orange during the Vietnam War in the 1960s to strip the leaves off trees that their enemies, the Vietcong, were using as cover. Since then, at least 150,000 children in Vietnam have been born with severe deformities, and perhaps a million people – both Vietnamese and American – have serious health problems (such as cancer) associated with the chemicals used in the Vietnam War.

This team are carrying out an emergency drill to prepare for biochemical attacks.

FINDING THE BALANCE

The international community of nations has begun to take steps to curb the damage that man is doing to nature, and increased publicity means that looking after the planet is now a major global concern. The Kyoto Protocol, devised in 1997 set out a programme for reducing emissions of CO_2 and other 'greenhouse gases', and takes into account the fact that it is easier for wealthier nations to control their pollution than poorer nations.

But not everyone is persuaded about the urgency or effectiveness of these measures. Many countries are still reluctant to sign up to the Kyoto Protocol or, if they already have, to take all the steps necessary to reduce polluting gases. The problem is that reducing greenhouse gas emissions requires a reduction in the use of fossil fuels – currently the main source of energy that helps to fuel

economic growth. Finding the right balance between man and nature requires constant research, monitoring, awareness campaigns, education and persuasion to make people (and governments) change their attitudes and lifestyles.

For the time being, natural disasters are only one part of the danger posed by man's impact on nature. But as our populations rise, and our demand for consumer goods accelerates, many scientists predict that global warming is set to continue. This brings an increased threat of violent weather, flooding, desertification, water shortages, famine and disease. Meanwhile, the accelerating frequency of natural disasters, such as hurricanes and flooding, may serve as early warnings of the dangers that will follow unless humans take notice and act before it is too late.

Nations gathered together in Kyoto, in Japan, in 1997 to try to address some of the environmental problems affecting our planet.

THE FUTURE

Humans will never be free from the threat of natural disasters. We can learn from the past and try to alter our lives to accommodate the threat that nature brings; but we don't know what the future holds. We know that there have been catastrophic events in the distant past that were far, far greater than anything that humans have ever seen. Will a disaster of this kind strike again? Only time will tell, and in the meantime we must learn to live alongside nature as best we can.

MEGA-DISASTERS

There have been colossal volcanic eruptions in the past that outweigh any disaster that has occurred in recent history. These eruptions spewed huge quantities of debris into the Earth's atmosphere, causing the sky to darken and global temperatures to sink, threatening countless life forms. About 74,000 years ago, Mount Toba in Sumatra, Indonesia, blew up with a force estimated at 10,000 times that of Mount St Helens in the US; it was probably the biggest eruption in two million years. Scientists estimate that perhaps 75 per cent of all plant species in the Northern Hemisphere died as a result, and man may have been pushed to the edge of extinction. Could this happen again?

The great extinctions of the past
In the distant past, life on Earth has been shattered by five episodes of massive extinctions. The greatest came at the end of the Permian period, 250 million years ago, when 90 per cent of life forms were made extinct. At the end of the Cretaceous period, 65.5 million years ago, about half of all life-forms, including the dinosaurs, were lost. Climate change appears to have been the cause, perhaps triggered by an asteroid collision. In such circumstances, only the toughest, most adaptable creatures can survive. In very severe climate change, the only life-form left might be bacteria, which are known to be capable of surviving extremes of heat and cold, and radical changes to the atmosphere.

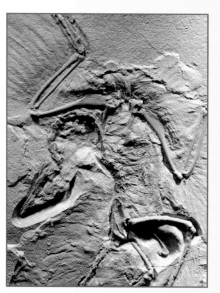

The Yellowstone super-volcano

Yellowstone Park, in central-western USA, is famous for its many varied volcanic wonders, including geysers and hot and brilliantly coloured mineral pools. But these are just the pretty surface phenomena of a huge volcanic force that lies beneath – and that force is growing, gradually pushing the land into a huge dome. In some places the land has risen 70 centimetres over the last century. There is serious concern that Yellowstone could turn into a colossal 'super-volcano', capable of exploding with such massive force that it would obliterate large areas of the USA and – through its air-borne debris – dramatically alter the climate of the world, causing global temperatures to fall, and plunging the world into a prolonged winter. Quite when and if this will happen remains a mystery.

The Earth's orbit around the Sun is not entirely regular and this means that, over time, the Earth goes through cycles of warming and cooling. During periods called 'Ice Ages', the polar ice caps grow larger, and freezing conditions spread outwards, covering regions that usually have a temperate climate, such as Europe and North America. The last Ice Age ended about 10,000 years ago, causing the extinction of various large mammals, such as mammoths, because their habitat changed. According to the known cycles of heating and cooling, the Earth is due for another Ice Age. The fact that the Earth is currently getting warmer fuels the argument that man, not nature, is responsible for the recent increase in temperatures on planet Earth.

Apocalypse now

Some scientists predict that if humans continue to pump the atmosphere full of carbon dioxide, the reduction of oxygen in the air will cause a mass extinction. 'Superbugs' – dangerous bacteria or viruses resistant to treatment – could also emerge and cause a lethal, worldwide pandemic endangering the entire human race.

In the past, the Earth has been hit by meteorites and asteroids hurtling from outer space. In 1908, an asteroid about 80 metres across plunged into the remote region of Tunguska, in Siberia, Russia, with a massive explosion that burnt and flattened 2,000 km² of forest. Fortunately, the area was virtually uninhabited – but it is easy to imagine what would happen if a similar asteroid hit a heavily populated area.

Most of the Earth's surface is not heavily populated: indeed, the greater part of it is covered by sea. But even a major impact in the sea is dangerous: it could set off a mega-tsunami. Large-scale impacts of this kind have occurred about once every hundred years; smaller ones about every 20 years. Are we in danger of another?

Larger asteroids, measuring two kilometres or more across, could strike with the force of thousands of nuclear bombs. According to widely-held theories, large asteroids of the past have radically altered the climate of the Earth, destroying the existing habitat, and causing the extinction of numerous animal species. A crater in Mexico suggests that the Earth was hit by an asteroid measuring about ten kilometres in diameter around 65 million years ago: such an impact would cause an explosion many millions of times more powerful than any nuclear bomb, and alter the atmosphere with vast clouds of dust and gas, plunging the Earth into a prolonged winter. Other similar craters, dating from about the same time, have been found off the east coast of England, in the Ukraine, and off the west coast of India, indicating that the Earth was hit by a number of large meteorites and asteroids. It is now widely believed that the extinction of the dinosaurs was caused by an asteroid collision, which caused clouds of dust to severely pollute the atmosphere.

This crater in Mexico is believed to have been caused by an asteroid that collided with the Earth around 65 million years.

Future collisions

Asteroid impacts could occur in the future and would give little warning. There are several hundred known 'near-Earth asteroids' in space. One, called 4581 Asclepius, measuring 300 metres in diameter, missed the Earth by 400,000 kilometres in 1989: this sounds a lot, but it passed through the precise position where the Earth had been just six hours before.

Astronomers estimate that collisions with asteroids larger than five kilometres in diameter take place approximately every ten million years or so. The chances of this occurring in our lifetime is remote. To give another perspective, the human species has only existed in any recognisable form for a mere two million years.

We should also take note that humans love to speculate about the destruction of planet Earth. In the distant past – and indeed among some people today too – visions of destruction were connected to religious beliefs. In the 19th century, scientists were sure that life on Earth would be destroyed by freezing as a result of a 'universal winter' caused by the collapse of the Sun. In the

Will we never learn?

Earthquakes, volcanic eruptions, hurricanes, tropical cyclones, tornadoes – these disasters all occur in the same places, repeatedly. What makes people continue to live in such places – in San Francisco, Los Angeles, Tokyo, on the coasts that have already been devastated by tsunamis? They know the dangers, but seem determined to take the risk.

One reason is that people have historically lived in these areas. Everything is set up to sustain human life there: buildings, roads, commerce, jobs, networks of family and friends. It seems easier to stay in such places, repair the damage, and face the risk of occasional disaster, than to move away completely.

In some parts of the world, measures are being taken to reduce the threat of natural disasters – such as constructing earthquake-resistant buildings in earthquake zones, or installing tsunami-warning equipment at sea in zones where undersea earthquakes occur. Evacuation procedures – in Bangladesh as well as Florida – have also improved. Since the disastrous floods of 1953, the Netherlands has built an ingenious system of sea defences along its coasts (the Delta Project); London has its Thames Barrier to defend against exceptionally high tides. Some lessons have been learnt about the dangers of building over wetlands and floodplains, which are historically prone to flooding. Tree-felling has been controlled in some areas where soil erosion has caused flooding. And tree planting in West Africa and China has had a dramatic impact on desertification and even led to the greening of the desert in some areas. But these are relatively modest gestures. In truth, humans have no real defence against the really big natural disasters, and because they insist on living in the zones where earthquakes, volcanic eruptions and hurricanes occur, disasters in the future are likely to get worse (in terms of human loss), not better.

period after the Second World War, an all-out nuclear war seemed to threaten human annihilation. Now the new vision of man's destruction is global warming.

LIVING ALONGSIDE NATURE

For the time being, we can only cope with what we know on a practical day-to-day basis. For our future, in as far as we can see it and predict it, we have to accept that natural disasters will happen; there is no way of avoiding them. The question is not if, but when – and what kind of measures can be taken to minimise their impact. We have recovered from disasters in the past, and we will continue to show resilience to the disasters of the future. We must learn from the past, first to avoid unnecessary disasters, and second to handle new disasters better when they occur. Only that way will we come close to living in harmony with our volatile natural world.

CHRONOLOGY

c.72,000 BC – Mount Toba in Indonesia erupted in the worst volcanic explosion of the last two million years.

AD 79 – The catastrophic eruption of Vesuvius (near modern Naples, in Italy) destroyed Pompeii and Herculaneum and killed some 3,500 people, although many citizens had evacuated.

1556 – The deadliest known earthquake hit central China, killing approximately 830,000 people.

1755 – An earthquake followed by a tsunami destroyed Lisbon, the capital of Portugal, killing about 100,000 people (about a third of the city's population).

1780 – 'The Great Hurricane' struck Martinique, Barbados and St Eustatius, killing 22,000.

1815 – Mount Tambora, Indonesia, erupted killing 12,000. A further 80,000 died from the resulting famine and disease.

1826–37 – The Second Cholera Pandemic spread around the world from India, killing millions (7,000 in London; 25,000 in Ireland; 50,000 in New York).

1857 – 107,000 people were killed by an earthquake in Tokyo, Japan.

1876–9 – Some nine million people died in China as a result of the worst recorded drought and famine in history.

1887 – The Huang He (Yellow River) in China flooded, resulting in the deaths of 1.5 million people.

1896 – A tsunami hit the coast of north-east Honshu, Japan, killing 27,000.

1900 – 12,000 people were killed when a hurricane hit the coastal city of Galveston, Texas, USA.

1902 – The eruption of Mont Pelée in Martinique, French West Indies, wiped out almost the entire population of the capital, Saint-Pierre (36,000 people).

1908 – 160,000 people died in an earthquake in southern Italy and Sicily.

1911 – A flood on the Yangtze River killed 200,000 in the region of Shanghai.

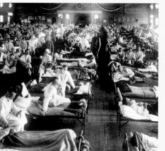

1918–19 – The 'Spanish flu' pandemic killed at least 25 million people worldwide.

1920 – 180,000 people died in an earthquake in Xining, Gansu Province, China.

1923 – 140,000 died in an earthquake in Tokyo, Japan.

1927 – The 'Great Mississippi Flood' covered an area the size of Ireland with up to 10 metres of water, displaced 700,000 people and killed 246.

1931 – Three million people died in China in floods from the Huang He (Yellow River) and the Yangtze River.

1932 – 70,000 died in an earthquake in Lanzhou, Gansu Province, China.

1932–40 – The American Midwest suffered a disastrous drought, resulting in the 'Dust Bowl', which rendered vast areas of farmland useless.

1935 – 60,000 people died in an earthquake that hit Quetta, Pakistan.

1939 – 75,000 died in an earthquake at Chillán, in Chile, and along the country's coastline.

1954 – 40,000 people died in a flood at Wuhan, Hubei Province, China.

1960 – The Great Chilean Earthquake (9.5 on the Richter scale) killed 3,000 people, most from the resulting tsunami that hit Hawaii 10,000 km away.

1963 – 22,000 died in the tropical cyclone that hit Chittagong, Bangladesh.

1970 – 500,000 were killed by a tropical cyclone that hit Bhola, Bangladesh.

1976 – The most devastating earthquake of modern times hit Tangshan, Hebei Province, China. According to official figures 242,000 died, but unofficial estimates put the total at twice or three times this figure.

1984–5 – A long drought (from 1981) in East Africa caused widespread starvation in Ethiopia, which is thought to have killed more than one million people.

1985 – 22,000 people died in Armero, Colombia, and neighbouring villages as a mudslide crashed down from the Nevado del Ruiz volcano.

1988 – Bangladesh suffered its worst flood on record after monsoon rains, covering two-thirds of the country, killed 5,000, and made 21 million people homeless.

1989 – Bangladesh suffered the biggest ever death toll from a tornado: up to 1,300 people were killed.

1991 – 139,000 died as a tropical cyclone hit Sandwip Island, near Chittagong, Bangladesh (see 1963).

1991 – In the Philippines, Mount Pinatubo erupted, but an evacuation saved all but 1,000 people.

1993 – In April–October, the Rivers Mississippi and Missouri spilled over their banks, causing the worst flood in the US since 1927.

1995 – An earthquake in Osaka Bay, Japan, shook the city of Kobe and killed 6,000.

1998 – Hurricane Mitch devastated Honduras and Nicaragua, killing 18,000.

1999 – 19,000 people died in an earthquake in Izmit, northwestern Turkey.

2003 – An earthquake killed 26,000 in Bam, Iran.

2004 – An earthquake followed by a tsunami wrought devastation in Indonesia, Thailand, Sri Lanka and India, killing some 280,000 people.

2005 – Hurricane Katrina devastated New Orleans and surrounding areas, killing more than 1,300 people.

2005 – An earthquake measuring 7.6 on the Richter scale hit Pakistan (epicentre in Kashmir), killing over 80,000 people.

45

ORGANISATIONS AND GLOSSARY

CARE – Co-operative for Assistance and Relief Everywhere (CARE) is a major charitable organisation, which brings help through aid projects and emergency relief around the world. It was founded in the USA in 1945, but is now based in Brussels.

European Union (EU) – This grouping of 25 European countries originated in 1951 when six countries agreed to promote peace and prosperity through trading and political agreements. The European Commission (the main policy-making body of the EU), based in Brussels, has a dedicated Humanitarian Aid Office called ECHO, which distributes large sums of money and aid (such as food) to countries in crisis, in particular following natural disasters.

Food and Agriculture Organisation (FAO) – This branch of the United Nations, based in Rome, specialises in food production, particularly in the Third World, with a special dedication to preventing famine. It helps to set up new farming initiatives, for example.

Médicins Sans Frontières (MSF) – Also known as Doctors Without Borders in English-speaking countries, MSF was founded originally by French doctors in 1971, but is now a large and respected international organisation. Volunteer doctors and medics, supported by donations, travel the world – particularly the Third World – to bring medical aid to whoever needs it, often in emergencies, regardless of their race, religion or political background.

Office for the Co-ordination of Humanitarian Affairs (OCHA) – This is the main co-ordinating agency of the United Nations dealing with natural disasters and other emergencies. A key figure is the Emergency Relief Co-odinator, the post to which Jan Egeland of Norway was appointed in 2003. OCHA is based in New York, USA, and Geneva, Switzerland.

Oxfam International – This major charity was founded in 1942 as the Oxford Committee for Famine Relief. It is now one of the world's leading charities, working in more than 100 countries to alleviate poverty and suffering, including that caused by natural disasters.

Red Cross – The International Red Cross and Red Crescent Movement brings together 181 national groups with the aim of organising relief missions in large-scale emergencies. The International Committee of the Red Cross was founded originally in 1859 in Switzerland to bring assistance to sick and wounded soldiers; it still serves as a neutral agency in wartime, and provides aid to refugees, but also plays a leading role in relief work after natural disasters.

Save the Children – Founded in Britain in 1919, Save the Children is a leading charity dedicated to emergency relief and long-term aid programmes focusing on the needs of children. Its international alliance combines 27 national organisations and works in more than 110 countries.

United Nations (UN) – An international organisation founded in 1945 to promote peace, security and economic development, the UN is composed of most of the countries of the world. Natural disasters are dealt with by its Office for the Co-ordination of Humanitarian Affairs (see below left).

World Food Programme (WFP) – This United Nations agency distributes emergency food to the victims of natural disasters, as well as to long-term refugees. Its headquarters are in Rome, Italy.

World Heath Organisation (WHO) – Based in Geneva, Switzerland, the WHO deals with global health issues, especially infectious diseases and epidemics. It co-ordinates efforts to tackle diseases such as AIDS, malaria and SARS, and monitors world trends.

Asteroid – A lump of rock or ice in space is called an asteroid if it is larger than about 50 metres in diameter.

Avian flu – This deadly type of flu virus infects birds, both wild and domestic (such as chickens); it is named after the Latin for bird *avis*. It can sometimes infect humans and if it mutates (changes) so that it can pass from human to human, it becomes extremely dangerous. The strain known as H5N1 is particularly feared.

Cyclone – In weather, a circulating pattern of air around an area of low pressure is known as a cyclone (or a depression). It can often bring stormy weather. Very severe cyclones (with wind speeds of more than 120 kph) are referred to as 'hurricanes' in the North Atlantic and 'typhoons' in China and the north Pacific.

Delta – Sometimes, as a river reaches its estuary to flow into the sea, it splits into numerous channels to form a delta. Low-lying and dominated by water, deltas are particularly vulnerable to flooding, as witnessed in the Ganges-Brahmaputra Delta in Bangladesh and India, the world's largest delta.

Earthquake – The sudden violent shaking of the ground, called an earthquake, is caused by movement of the Earth's crust along the line where two tectonic plates meet. A minor earthquake that causes little or no damage is sometimes called an earth tremor.

Epicentre – The epicentre is the place on the Earth's surface that lies directly above the heart or 'focus' of an earthquake, and the place where, usually, its destructive force is at its greatest.

Fossil fuels – Most of our main fuels for making energy – oil, natural gas, coal – come from ancient deposits of organic materials (plants and animals) laid down in the surface of the Earth millions of years ago. When fossil fuels are burnt they give off carbon dioxide gas, one of the main 'greenhouse gases' held responsible for global warming.

Meteoroid – A lump of rock or ice in space is called a meteoroid if it is less than about 50 metres in diameter. If it enters the Earth's atmosphere and burns up (as a 'falling star') it is called a meteor; if it reaches the ground, it is called a meteorite.

Monsoon – The word monsoon is often associated with rain, but it is in fact a wind that blows across southern Asia at different seasons. The original Arabic word *mawsim* meant 'season'. When a monsoon blows from the south-west, from about April to October, it brings heavy rains – sometimes very heavy rains, which cause flooding.

Richter scale – The scale by which earthquakes are measured is named after its inventor, the American seismologist Charles Richter. The scale does not rise in a straight line: instead, an earthquake of the magnitude of 6 is ten times more powerful than an earthquake that measures 5, which is ten times more powerful than an earthquake that measures 4, and so on. Any earthquake measuring a magnitude of 6 or more is likely to cause severe damage.

Seismology – The word for the scientific study of earthquakes is derived from the ancient Greek for an earthquake, *seismos*. 'Seismic' is an adjective used to describe any kind of shaking of the Earth's surface associated with earthquakes or volcanoes.

Tectonic plate – The massive, moving plates into which the Earth's crust is divided are called tectonic plates, from the ancient Greek word *tektonikos* meaning 'relating to construction'.

Tsunami – A massive wave caused by an undersea earthquake or volcanic eruption. In the past, these devastating waves were known as 'tidal waves', but they have nothing to do with tides. Today, the term tsunami is preferred, which comes from the Japanese meaning 'harbour wave' (because a harbour might be destroyed even though fishermen had noticed nothing at sea).

INDEX

48

Photo Credits:
Abbreviations: l-left, r-right, b-bottom, t-top, c-centre, m-middle. Front cover main – Comstock. Front cover ml, 10bl, 16tl, 34tr, 36mr – Digital Vision. Front cover c, 1m, 1r, 2ml, 2bl, 4tl, 8-9, 9br, 23tr, 28mc, 37tr, 38ml, 40tl, 42tl – Corbis. Front cover mr, 14ml – Win Henderson/FEMA. 1l, 3tr, 12tr, 15tr, 15br, 17tr, 20mb, 21tr, 25tr, 27bl, 39tl, 45br – U.S. Navy. 2-3, 6m, 7bl, 41tr – Photodisc. 4-5, 10mr – World Food Programme. 5tr, 15tl, 17bl, 22mr, 26tr – Marty Bahamonde/FEMA. 6tr, 32mr, 33bl – WHO/P. Virot. 8mr – Library of Congress. 11br – Mark Wolfe/FEMA. 12br – Myles Chilton/WPN. 14tr, 35bl, 43mr, 45tl – Andrea Booher/FEMA. 14bl – Barry Voight. 15bl – ACT. 16br – REUTERS/Pierre Holtz. 18bl, 27br, 34br – Corel. 19mr – David Rydevik. 20tl – Jocelyn Augustino/FEMA. 22br – Marvin Nauman/FEMA. 24br – Mark Lawhead. 28tr – www.istockphoto.com/Matt Matthews. 29tr – Disasterman Ltd. 30br – www.istockphoto.com /Lou Oates. 31tr, 35ml, 35mr, 37bl – NASA's Earth Observatory. 31br – www.istockphoto.com/Kate Shephard. 33tr – Michael Rieger/FEMA. 37mr – www.istockphoto.com/Chris Schmidt. 39br – © European Community. 40mb – www.istockphoto.com/Bob Ainsworth. 42m – www.istockphoto.com. 44tr – www.istockphoto.com/Bill Gruber. 44m – Courtesy of the National Museum of Health and Medicine, Armed Forces Institute of Pathology, Washington D.C.